SECOND EDITION 0

Student's Book



# SUPER MINDS

Herbert Puchta · Peter Lewis-Jones

CAMBRIDGE
UNIVERSITY PRESS

# Map of the book

## 5 My food (pages 50 – 59)

What food do we eat?

| Vocabulary | Language focus | Story / Value | Think and learn |
|---|---|---|---|
| Food | • *I like / I don't like …*<br>• *Do you like … ?* | **Story**<br>The cakes<br>**Value**<br>Sharing | Science: Fruit and vegetables |
| ▶ Song: I like you | | ▶ Creativity: Create that! | ▶ Revision: Think back |

## 6 My town (pages 60 – 69)

What's in your town?

| Vocabulary | Language focus | Story / Value | Think and learn |
|---|---|---|---|
| Places in a town | • *There's / There are …*<br>• *Where's the … ? It's there.* | **Story**<br>The toy shop<br>**Value**<br>Being kind | Geography: Maps and towns |
| ▶ Song: A really cool town | | ▶ Creativity: Do that! | ▶ Revision: Think back |

## 7 Jobs (pages 70 – 79)

What's a job?

| Vocabulary | Language focus | Story / Value | Think and learn |
|---|---|---|---|
| Jobs | • *He's/She's a …*<br>• *Is he/she a … ?* | **Story**<br>The teacher<br>**Value**<br>Appreciating others | Social science: Jobs inside and outside |
| ▶ Song: Helping me, helping you | | ▶ Creativity: Create that! | ▶ Revision: Think back |

## 8 My clothes (pages 80 – 89)

What clothes do we need?

| Vocabulary | Language focus | Story / Value | Think and learn |
|---|---|---|---|
| Clothes | • *I'm wearing …*<br>• *Is he/she wearing … ?* | **Story**<br>Hot or cold?<br>**Value**<br>Being prepared | Science: Different clothes |
| Song: It's cold! | | ▶ Creativity: Do that! | ▶ Revision: Think back |

## 9 My hobbies (pages 90 – 99)

What are hobbies?

| Vocabulary | Language focus | Story / Value | Think and learn |
|---|---|---|---|
| Hobbies | • *I'm + ing*<br>• *Are you + ing?* | **Story**<br>Guess what I'm doing?<br>**Value**<br>Saying sorry | Maths: Bar charts |
| Song: I'm having fun | | ▶ Creativity: Create that! | ▶ Revision: Think back |



Practice of creative thinking, critical thinking and cognitive skills

# Say Hello!

1 01 Listen and sing.

## 1 03 Listen and point. Say the names.

## 2 Ask and answer.

## 1 04 Listen and point. Listen and say the words.

## 2 Look and find. Say.

## 1 05 Listen and point. Listen and say the numbers.

## 2 Point and say. Count.

# Friends

**1** 06 Watch and listen to the story.

## 2 Find and colour. Say the colours.

# 1 My classroom

1 07 Listen and point. Say the words.

BIG QUESTION What's in my classroom?

2 08 Listen and chant.

## 1 09 Listen and point. Listen and stick.

1

2

3

4

## 2 10 Look, listen and say.

## 3 Work with a partner. Say and do.

1 11 Listen and sing.

2 Count the classroom objects and the children.

## 1 13 Listen and circle.

## 2 Watch and listen.

## 3 Play the game.

# The butterfly

**1** 14 Watch and listen to the story.

## 2 What's different? Look and circle.

# PATTERNS

Watch and listen.

1 15 Listen and point.

1

crayon

2

pen

3

rubber

2 Point and say the numbers.

1 2 3 4 5 ? 7 8 ? 10

1 2 3 ? 5 6 7 ? 9 10

3 16 Say what's next. Listen and check.

1

?

2

?

3

?

## 4 Choose and circle the next picture.

1 

2 

3 

4 

## 5 Project Create your own pattern. Say.

## Create that!

1 17 Listen and imagine. Then draw your picture.

2 Show your picture to your friend. Say.

## 1 Listen and point. Then say.

18

## 2 Listen and circle.

19

1 

2 

3 

4 

## 3 Draw the last picture.

1 

2 

# 2 My body

**1** 20 Listen and point. Say the words.

BIG QUESTION How do we move?

**2** 21 Listen and chant.

## 1 22 Listen to the monsters. Colour.

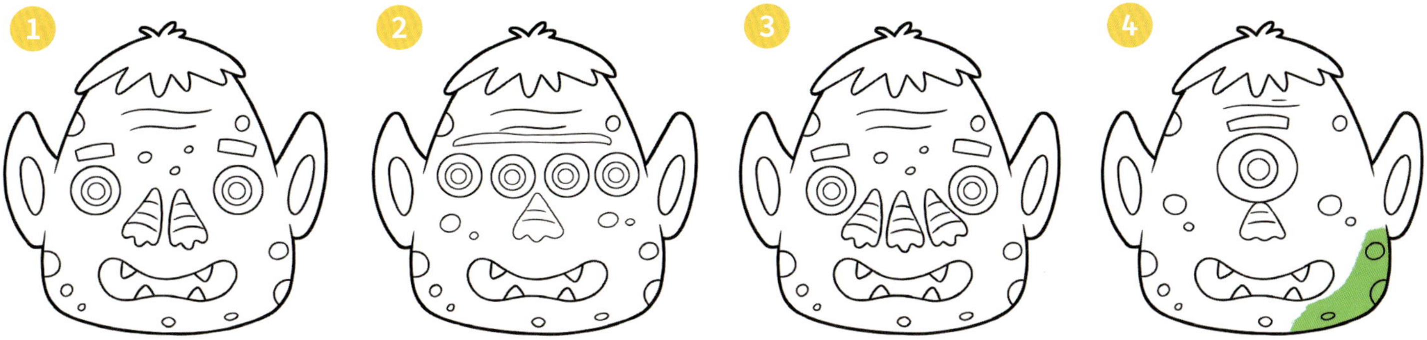


## 2 23 Look, listen and say.

## 3 Play the monster game.

## 1 24 Listen and sing.

## 2 Which monster? Say *chocolate* or *ice cream*.

1

2

3

4

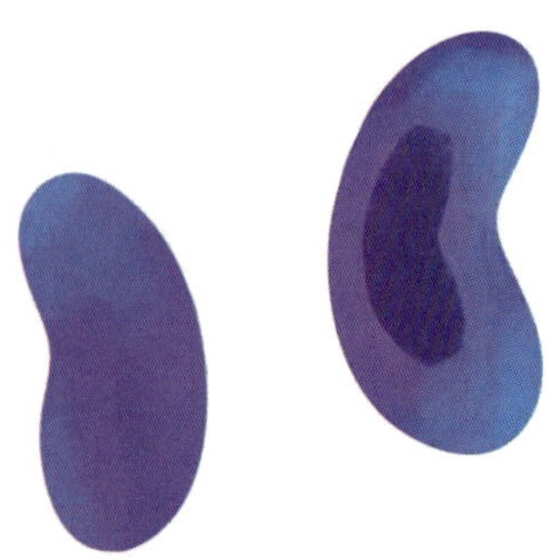

1 26 Listen and draw.

2 Watch and listen.

3 Draw a monster. Play *Ask the monster.*

# Great costumes!

**1** 27 Watch and listen to the story.

7

8

## 2 Find, count and stick.

1

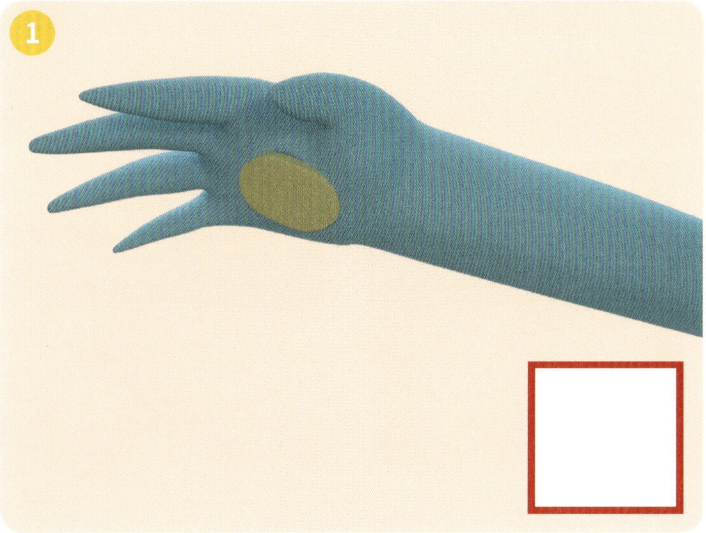

2

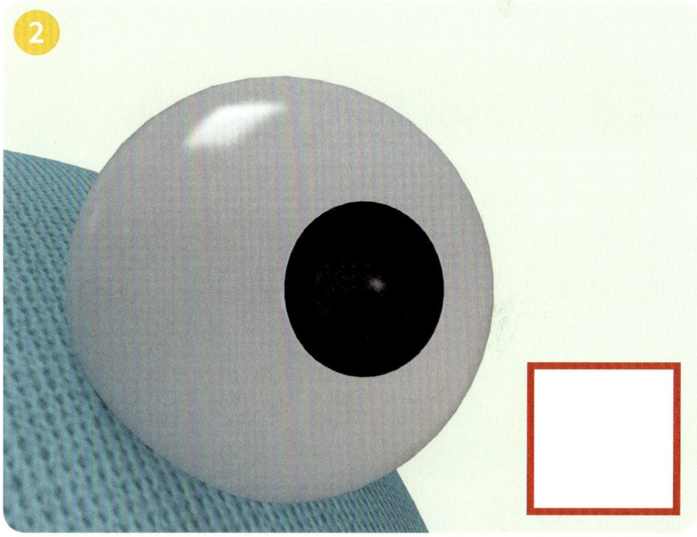

3

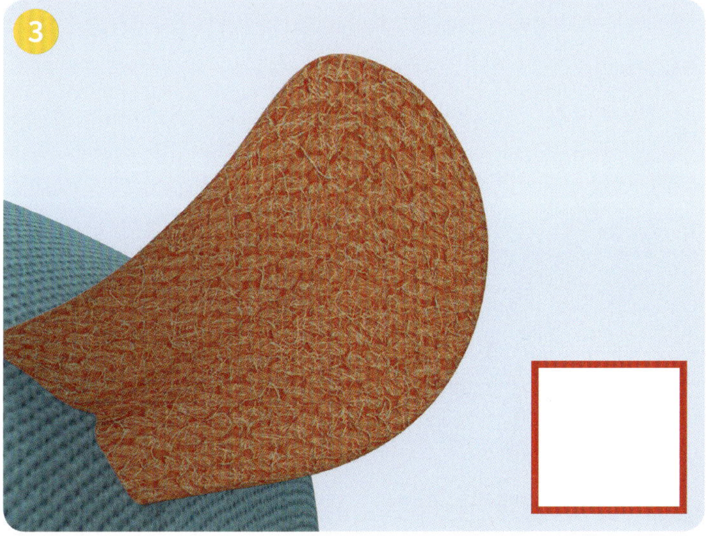

4

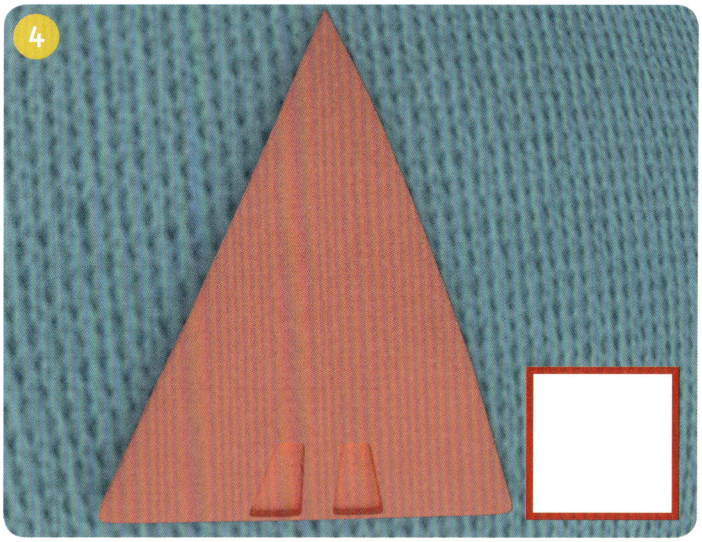

# OUR SKELETON

Watch and listen.

## 1 28 Listen and point.

1 
walk

2 
run

3 
wave

## 2 Look and match.

1 

2 

3 

4 

a 

b 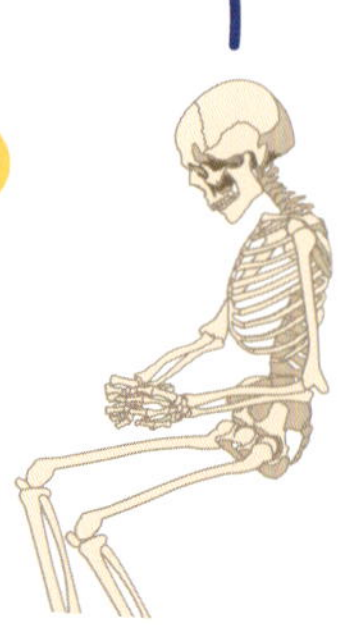

c 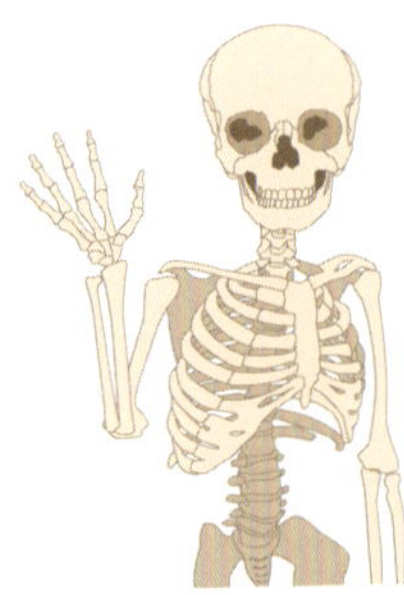

d 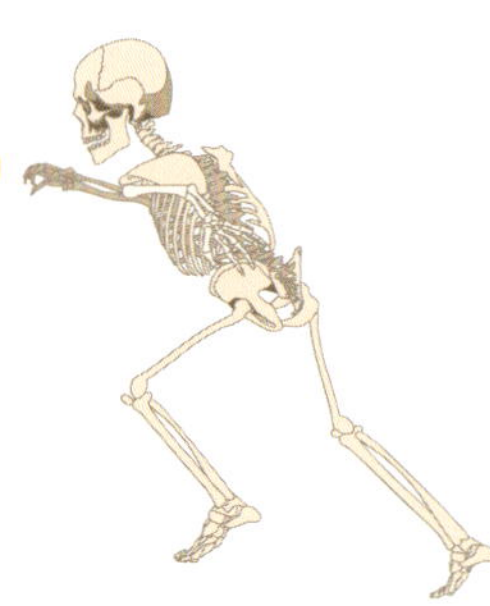

## 3 Look and say.

1

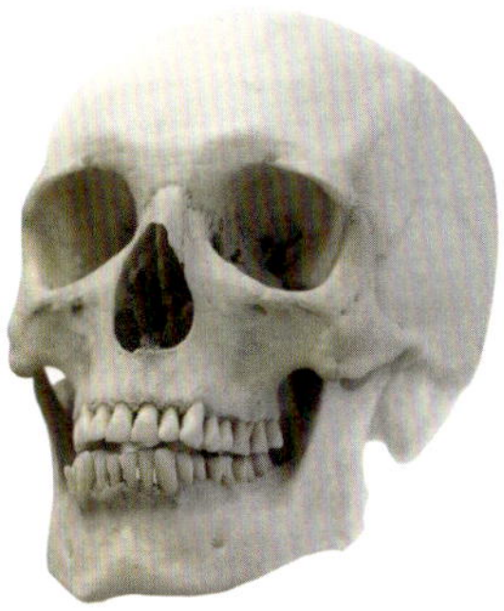

2

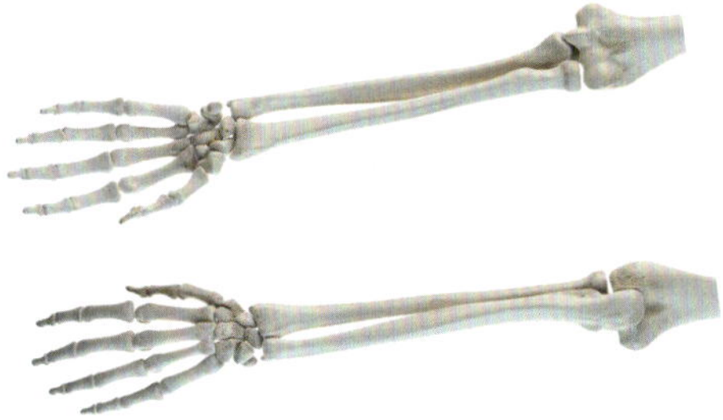

3

4

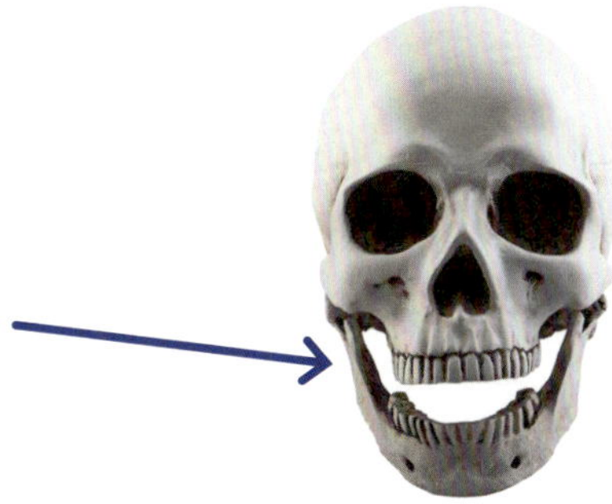

## 4 Project Draw three stick people. Show how they run, wave and sit.

**1** 29 Listen and act out with your teacher. Then listen again and match.

1 2 3 4 5 6

## 1 30 Listen and point. Then say.

## 2 31 Listen and colour.

## 3 Look and circle. Then say.

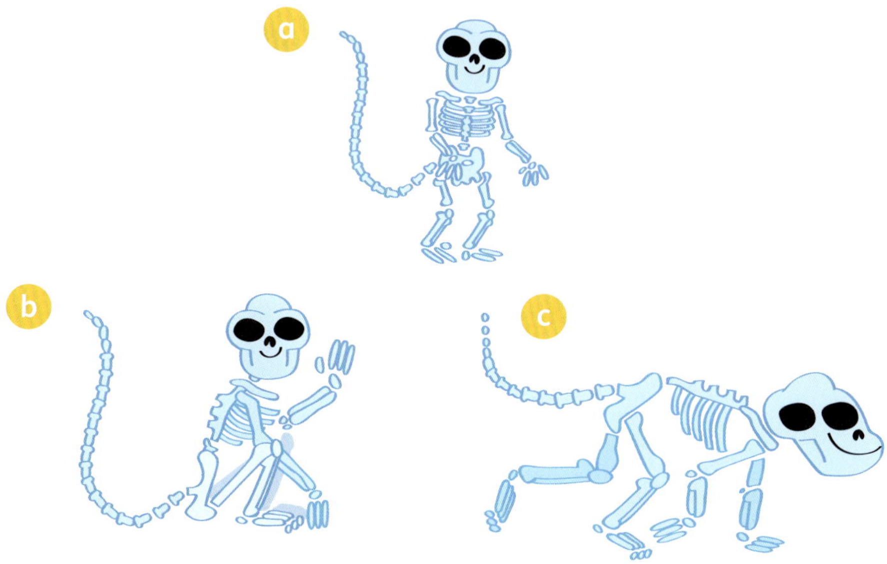

# 3 My family

1 32 Listen and point. Say the words.

BIG QUESTION What's a family?

2 33 Listen and chant.

## 1 Listen and circle the correct person.

## 2 Look, listen and say.

## 3 Draw your family. Point and say.

## 1 36 Listen and sing.

## 2 How many in each family? Look and count.

## 1 38 Listen and stick.

1

2

3

4

5

6

## 2 Watch and listen.

## 3 Ask and answer.

# Cool grandma

1 39 Watch and listen to the story.

7

8

## 2 Find and count. Draw how many.

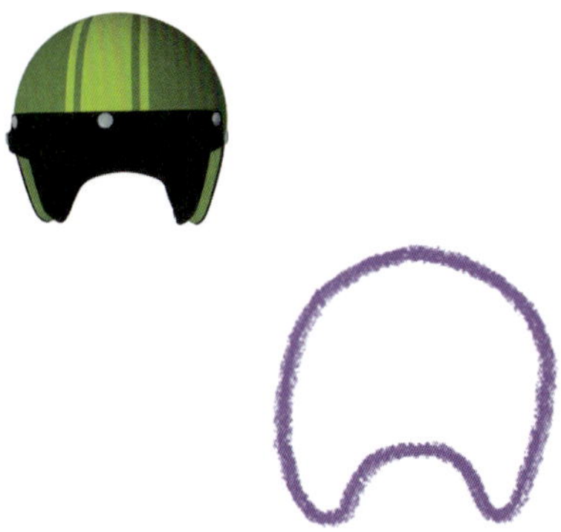

# An animal family

▶ Watch and listen.

## 1 🎧 40 Listen and point.

1

hen

2

dog

3

duck

4

cat

## 2 Look and match.

1

2

3

4

## 3 Look and circle the different animal.

1

2

3

## 4 Project Make an animal family. Say.

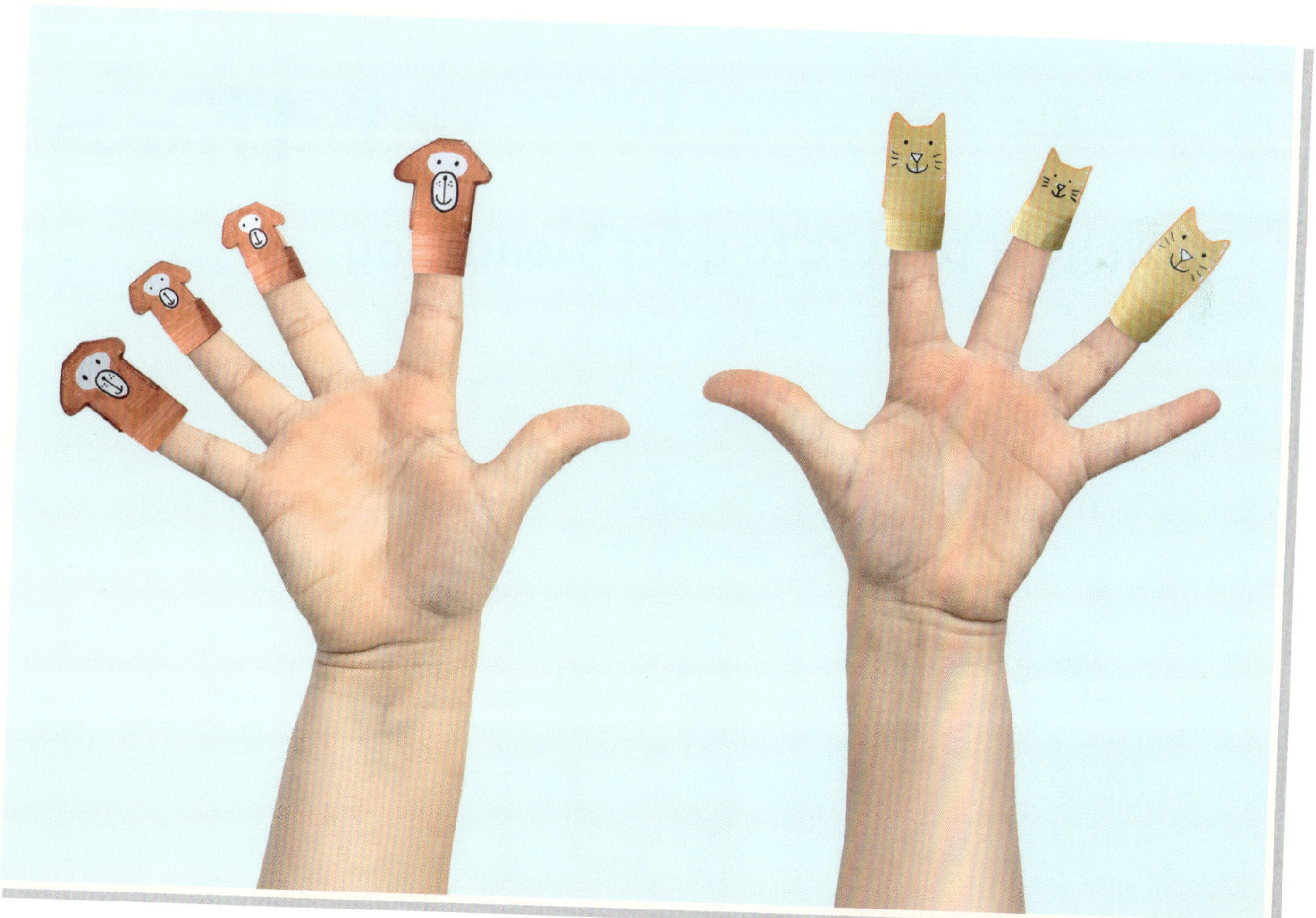

1 41 Listen and imagine. Then draw your picture.

2 Show your picture to your friend. Say.

## 1 Listen and point. Then say.

42

## 2 Listen and colour.

43

## 3 Look and circle the different animal.

# 4 At the zoo

1 44 Listen and point. Say the words.

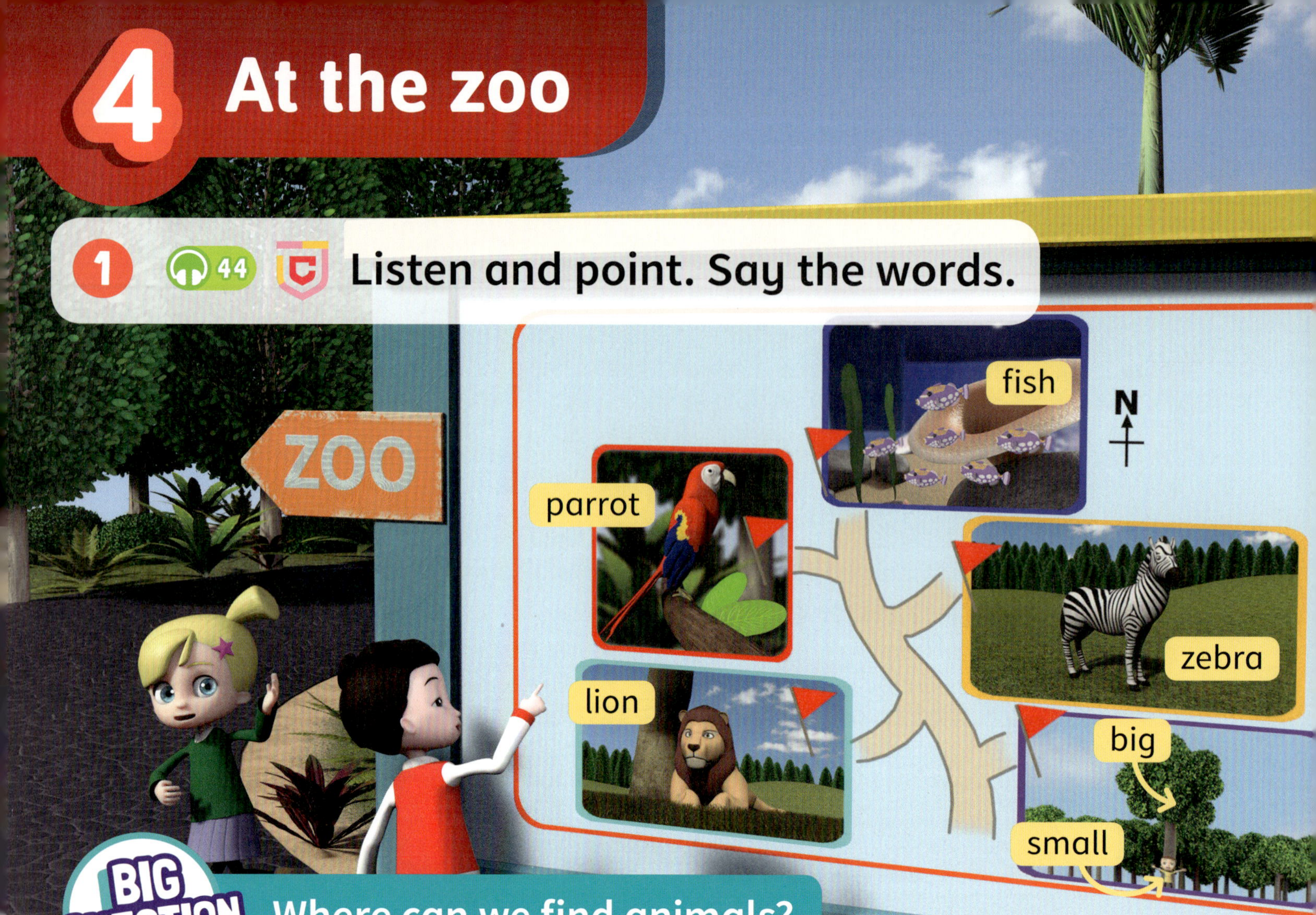


BIG QUESTION Where can we find animals?

2 45 Listen and chant.

## 1 46 Listen and stick.

## 2 47 Look, listen and say.

## 3 Complete the pictures. Point and say.

## 1 48 Listen and sing.

## 2 Find and circle the four animals in the song.

## 1 Listen and tick ☑.

## 2 Watch and listen.

## 3 Draw for you. Then ask and answer.

| | You | Friend |
|---|---|---|
| Favourite animal?  | | |
| Favourite colour?  | | |

1 51 Watch and listen to the story.

7

8

## 2 What's different? Look and circle.

Think and learn

# Animal habitats

Watch and listen.

**1** 52 Listen and point.

1 
monkey

2 
frog

3 
tree

4 
pond

5 
grassland

**2** Where do these animals live? Draw lines.

1 

2 

3 

a 

b 

c 

4 

5 

6 

## 3 Look and circle the wrong animal.

a

b

c

## 4 Project Make a puzzle for your friend.

## Do that!

**1** 53 Listen and act out with your teacher. Then listen again and match.

1 2 3 4 5 6

## 1 54 Listen and point. Then say.

## 2 55 Listen and number.

a

☐

b

☐

c

☐

d

1

## 3 Draw the missing animal. Then say.

1

2

# 5 My food

## 1 56 Listen and point. Say the words.

**BIG QUESTION** What food do we eat?

## 2 57 Listen and chant.

## 1 58 Listen and stick 😊 or 😞.

1

2

3

4

5

6

## 2 59 Look, listen and say.

## 3 Talk about food.

cake

tomatoes

milk

oranges

chocolate

pears

*I like (oranges). I don't like (milk).*

## 1 60 Listen and sing.

## 2 Look, think and draw  or .

1 62 Listen and draw 😊 or 😞.

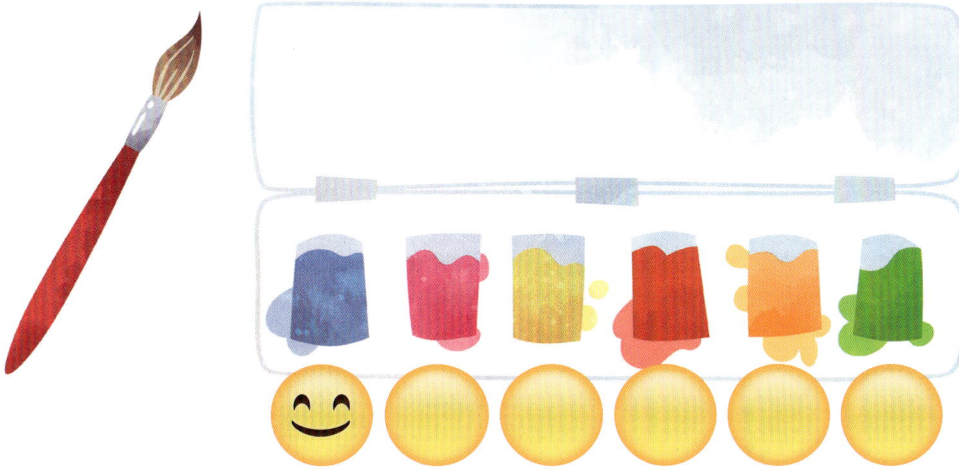

2 Watch and listen.

3 Ask and answer. Draw 😊 or 😞.

| | Me | My friend ______ | My friend ______ |
|---|---|---|---|
| pink | | | |
| blue | | | |
| green | | | |
| pears | | | |
| chocolate | | | |
| tomatoes | | | |

*Do you like (pink)? Yes, I do. / No, I don't.*

# The cakes

**1** 63 Watch and listen to the story.

## 2 Look and draw the cakes.

# Fruit and vegetables

Watch and listen.

1 64 Listen and point.

1 
potatoes

2 
carrots

3 
bananas

4 
ground

2 Where does our food come from? Draw lines.

1 

2 

## 3 Look and circle the wrong one.

1

2

## 4 Project Make a food picture. Say.

## Create that!

1 65 Listen and imagine. Then draw your picture.

2 Show your plate to your friend. Say.

## 1 Read and match.

1 

2 

3 

pear

cake

orange

## 2 Read and draw or .

1 

I don't like cake.

2 

Do you like chocolate?

Yes, I do.

## 3 Which food is different? Circle.

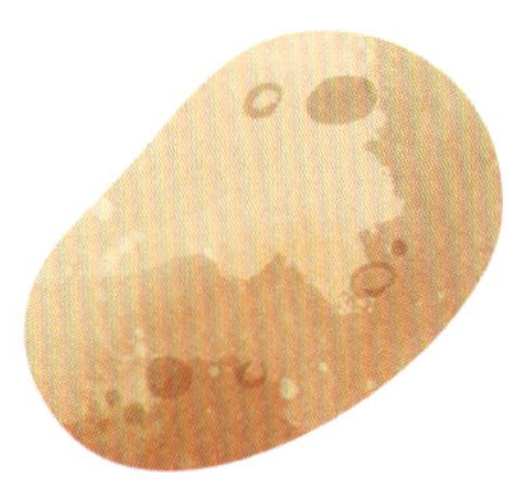

# 6 My town

## 1 66 Listen and point. Say the words.

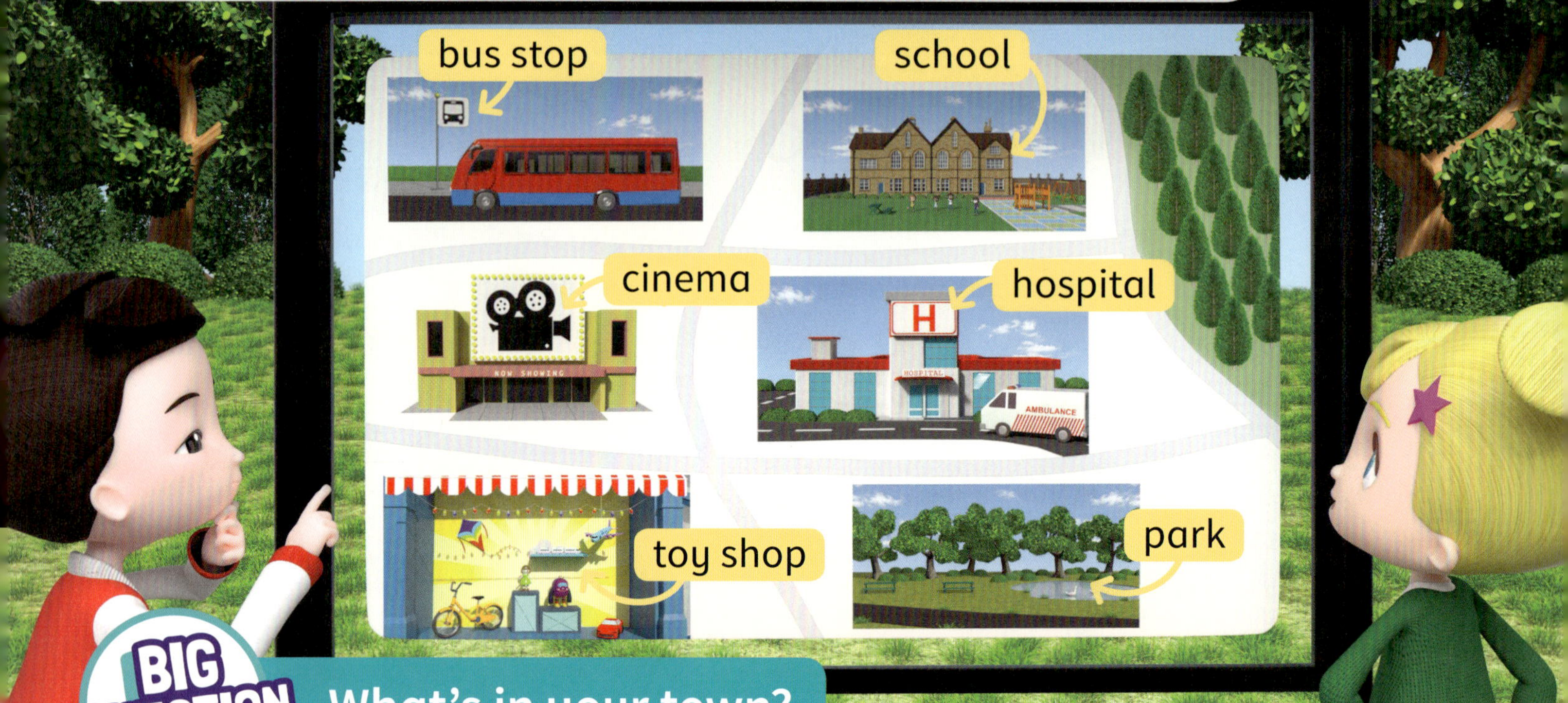


**BIG QUESTION** What's in your town?

## 2 67 Listen and chant.

## 1 68 Listen and match.

Will Lola Tom Flo

## 2 69 Look, listen and say.

## 3 Draw your town. Say.

## 1 70 Listen and sing.

## 2 Where do these people work? Point and say.

## 1 72 Listen and draw Max's route.

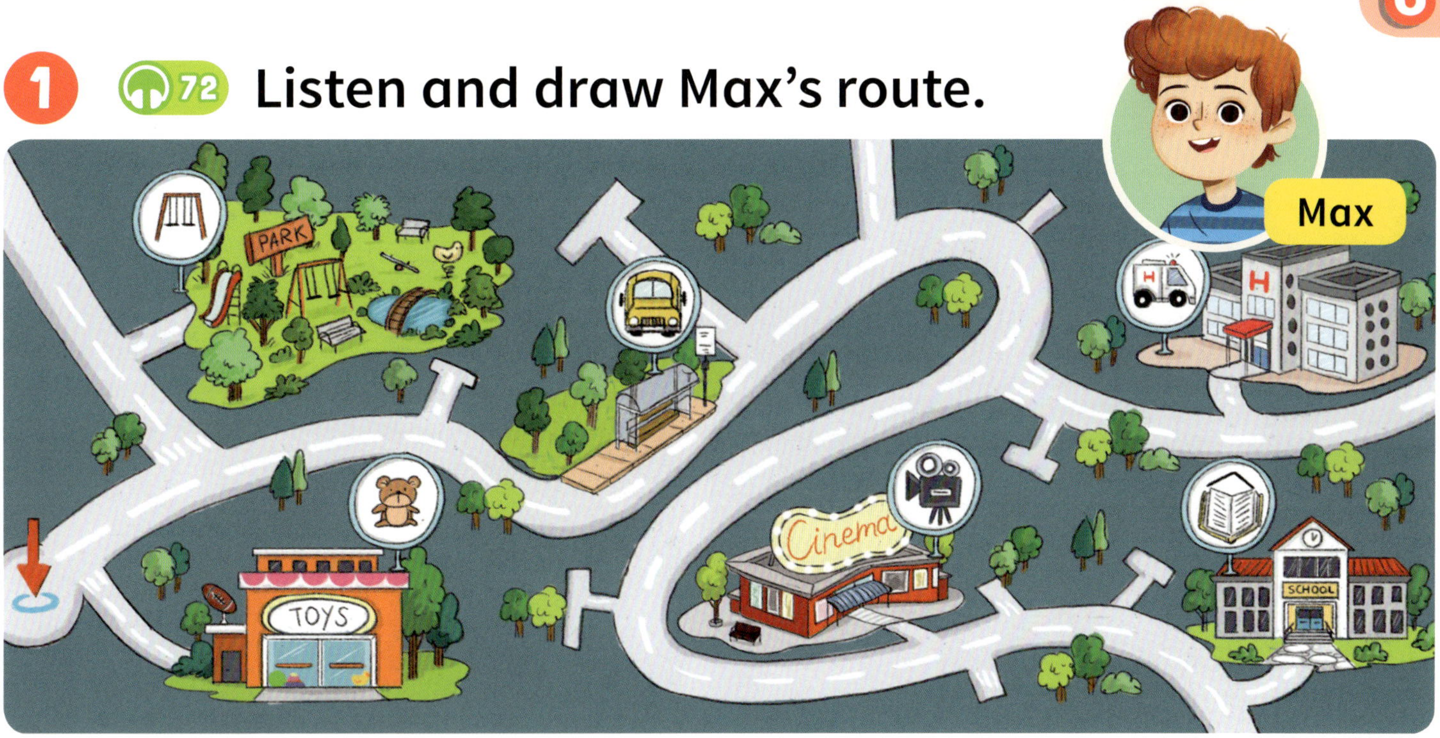


## 2 Watch and listen.

## 3 Ask a partner. Find and answer.

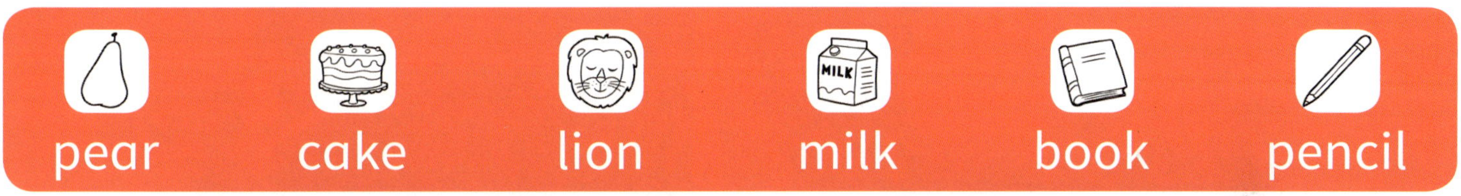

# The toy shop

**1** 73 Watch and listen to the story.

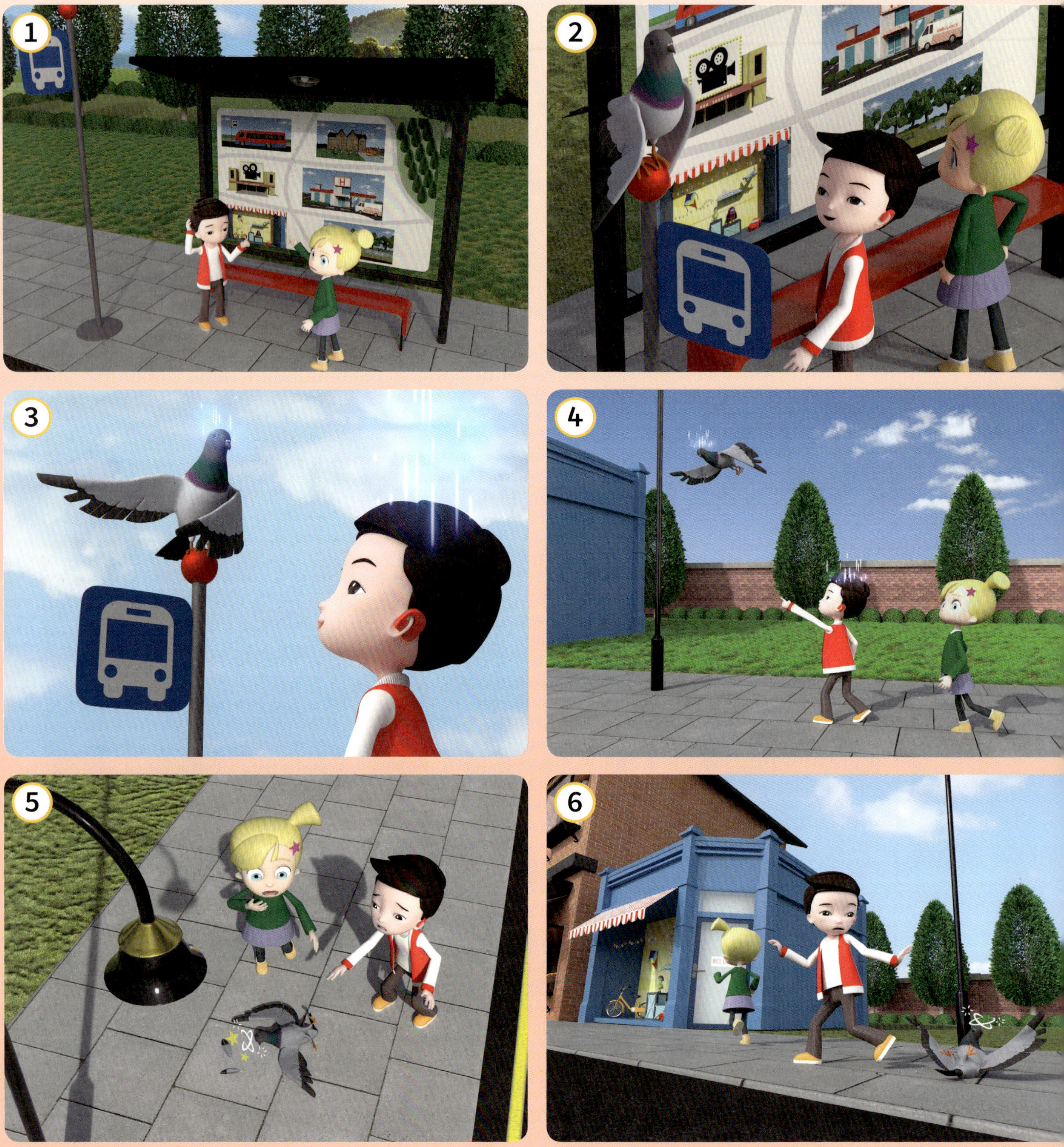

7

8

## 2 Look, find and write the picture number.

a

6

b

c

d

e

f

# Maps and towns

Watch and listen.

**1** 74 Listen and point.

1 
market

2 
café

3 
playground

4 
sports centre

5 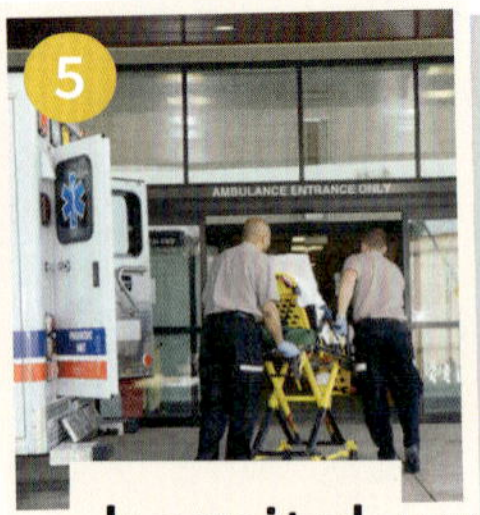
hospital

6 
cinema

**2** Look and match. Write the numbers.

a 
4

b 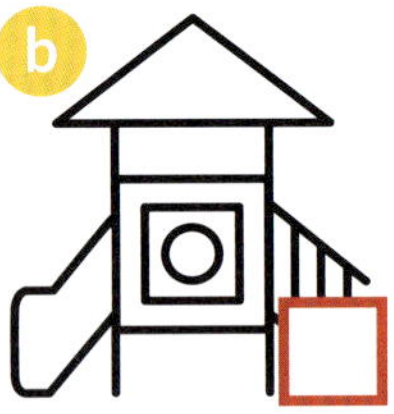

c 

d 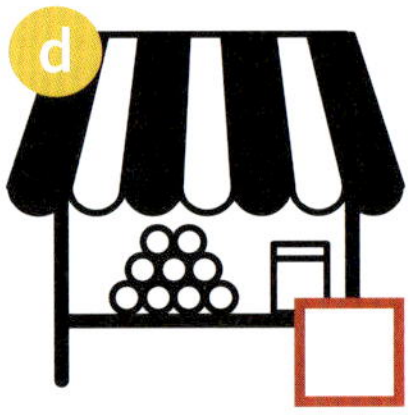

e 

f 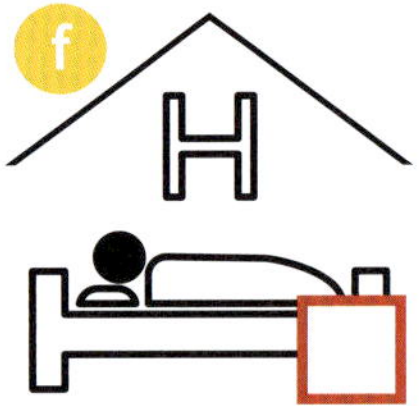

**3** Look and stick.

## 4 Draw symbols. Then say.

## 5 Project Make a map of your dream town.

1 75 Listen and act out with your teacher. Listen again and match.

1 2 3 4 5 6

## 1 Read and match.

1

2

3

4
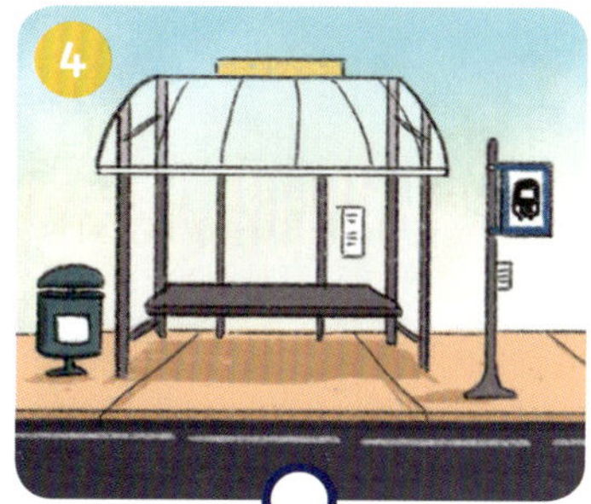

toy shop    cinema    bus stop    school

## 2 Write.

1
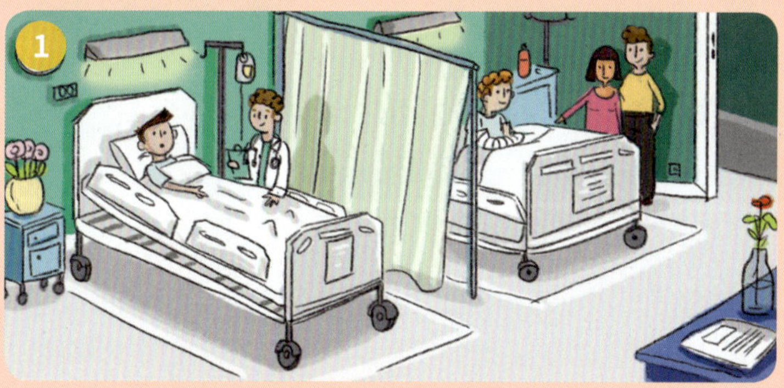

This is a ___ospital.

2

This is a ___ark.

## 3 Read and tick ☑ or cross ☒.

1
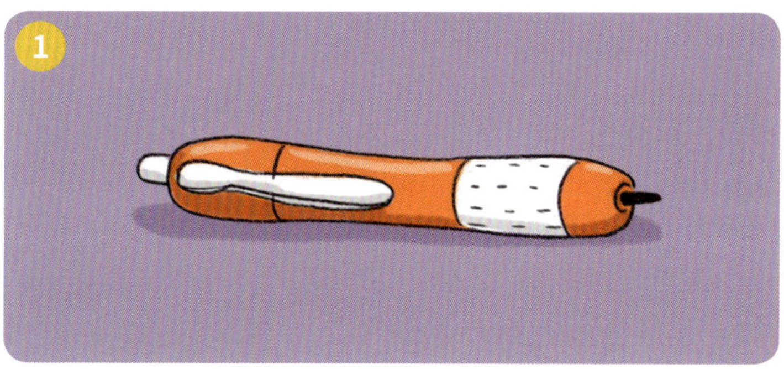

There's a pen. ☐

There are pen. ☐

2

There's four pens. ☐

There are four pens. ☐

# 7 Jobs

**1** 76 Listen and point. Say the words.

**BIG QUESTION** What's a job?

**2** 77 Listen and chant.

## 1 (78) Listen and tick ☑.

## 2 (79) Look, listen and say.

## 3 Look and draw lines. Say.

He's a police officer.

1 80 Listen and sing.

2 Mime a job for your partner to guess.
Wave and say *Hello* if they're correct!

## 1 Listen, read and tick ☑.

1

doctor ☐
gardener ☑

2

teacher ☐
doctor ☐

3

fire fighter ☐
police officer ☐

4

fire fighter ☐
vet ☐

## 2 Watch and listen.

## 3 Point. Ask and answer.

Is she a vet?

Yes, she is.

*Is he/she a (fire fighter)? Yes, he/she is. No, he/she isn't.*

# The teacher

**1** 83 Watch and listen to the story.

## 2 Look at picture 6. Circle four differences.

# JOBS INSIDE AND OUTSIDE

Watch and listen.

1 84 Listen and point.

1 farmer

2 shop assistant

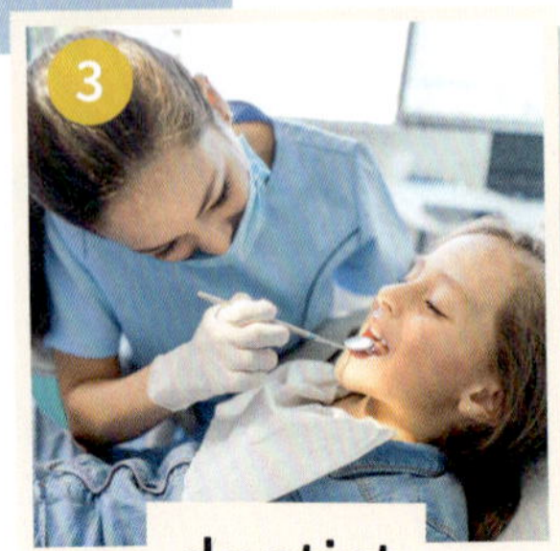
3 dentist

4 inside

5 outside

2 Look and stick.

**3** **Where do they work? Look and write *I* for *inside*, *O* for *outside* or *B* for *both*.**

**4** Project **Make a class poster. Say.**

He's a farmer.
He's outside.

1 85 Listen and imagine. Then draw your picture.

2 Show your picture to your friend. Say.

## 1 Read and match.

teacher fire fighter police officer doctor

## 2 Complete the words.

She' s a ___ardener.

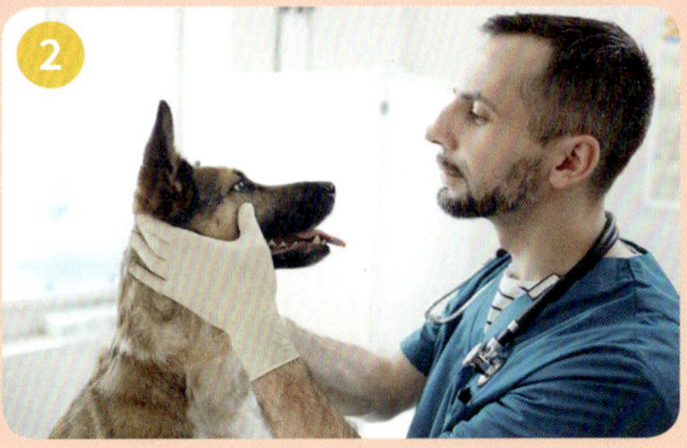

___ ___'s a vet.

___ ___ ___'s a ___ire fighter.

## 3 Read and tick ✓.

Is she a doctor?

Yes, she is. ☐

No, she isn't. ☐

Is he a police officer?

Yes, he is. ☐

No, he isn't. ☐

She's a …

police officer ☐

teacher. ☐

# 8 My clothes

**1** 86 Listen and point. Say the words.

**BIG QUESTION** What clothes do we need?

**2** 87 Listen and chant.

## 1 🎧 88 Listen and tick ☑.

1
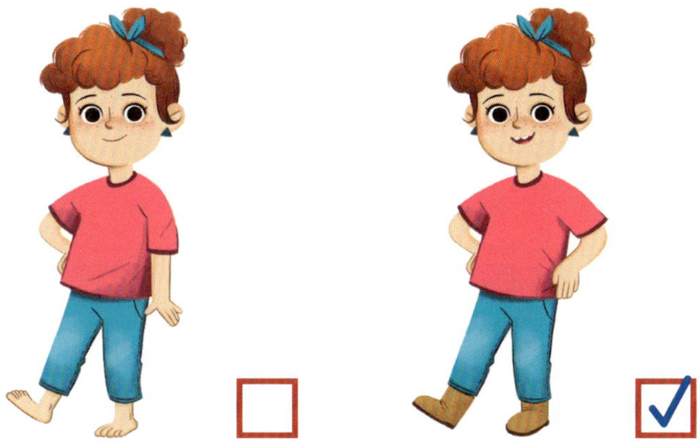

2

3

4

## 2 🎧 89 Look, listen and say.

## 3 Choose and colour your outfit. Say.

## 1 90 Listen and sing.

## 2 Read and number the clothes in order.

☐ scarf   1 jeans   ☐ coat   ☐ hat

## 1 Listen and stick.

92

Will Fran

## 2 Watch and listen.

## 3 Work with a partner. Play *Guess who?*

Is he wearing a scarf?

Yes, he is.

Ben Alex Tom Jill Eva Ann

# Hot or cold?

1 93 Watch and listen to the story.

## 2 Look and read. Tick ☑ Misty's clothes.

| |  |  |  |  |
|---|---|---|---|---|
| scarf | | | | |
| jeans | ✓ | | | |
| coat | | | | |
| hat | | | | |
| sweater | | | | |
| T-shirt | | | | |

# Different clothes

▶ Watch and listen.

1 🎧 94 Listen and point.

1 
soft

2 
hard

3 
cold

4 
hot

5 
belt

6 
sunglasses

2 Is it soft or hard? Draw lines.

1 

2 

3 

soft

hard

4 

5 

6 

3 Circle the items red for hot weather and blue for cold weather.

1 

2 

3 

4 

5 

6 

7 

8 

9 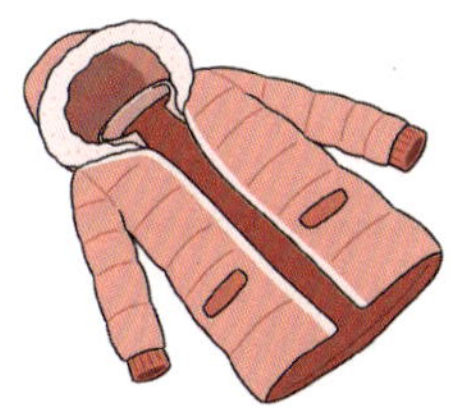

4 Project Draw clothes in a table.

| | soft | hard |
|---|---|---|
| hot |  |  |
| cold |  |  |

# Do that!

**1** 95 Listen and act out with your teacher.
Listen again and match.

1 2 3 4 5 6

## 1 Read and match.

1 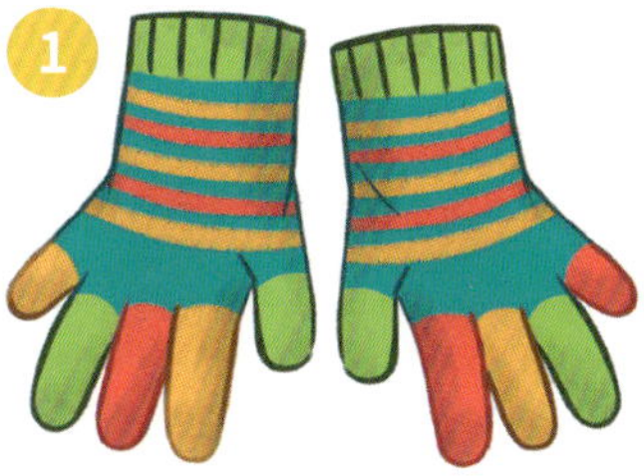

2 

3 

4 

coat gloves boots sweater

## 2 96 Listen and write *S* for *Sally*, *T* for *Tim* and *K* for *Kate*.

1  ☐

2  ☐

3  ☐

## 3 Look and circle *soft* or *hard*.

1 

soft
hard

2 

soft
hard

3 

soft
hard

4 

soft
hard

# 9 My hobbies

## 1 97 Listen and point. Say the words.

BIG QUESTION What are hobbies?

## 2 98 Listen and chant.

## 1 Listen and number. (99)

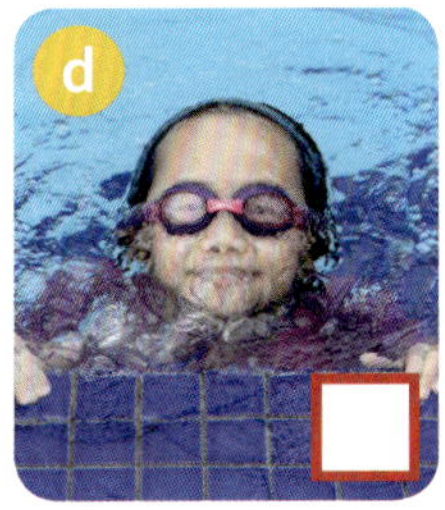

## 2 Look, listen and say. (100)

## 3 What's next? Look, draw and say.

I'm dancing!

1

2

3

## 1 101 Listen and sing.

## 2 Read, count the children and write the number.

How many children are …

| | | | |
|---|---|---|---|
| reading? | 2 | running? | |
| painting? | | swimming? | |
| dancing? | | playing football? | |

## 1 Listen and stick. (103)

## 2 Watch and listen.

## 3 Play the game.

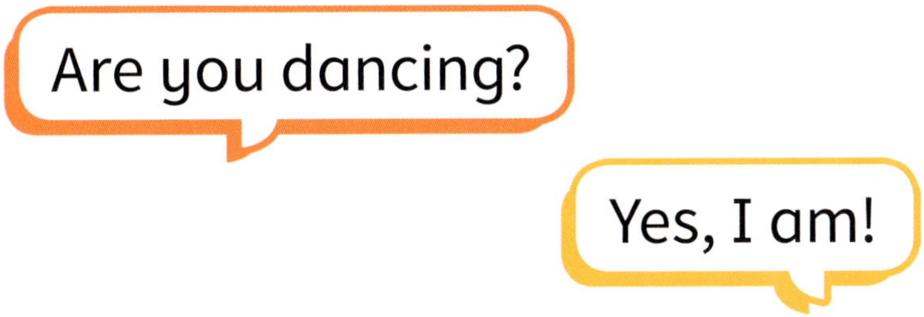

*Are you (swimming)? Yes, I am. / No, I'm not.*

# Guess what I'm doing?

1 104 Watch and listen to the story.

## 2 Look and write the words. Tick ☑ the activity from the story.

swim ~~dance~~ play football read

1 ☐

dance

2 ☐

______

3 ☐

______

4 ☐

______

# BAR CHARTS

Watch and listen.

**1** 105 Listen and point.

1 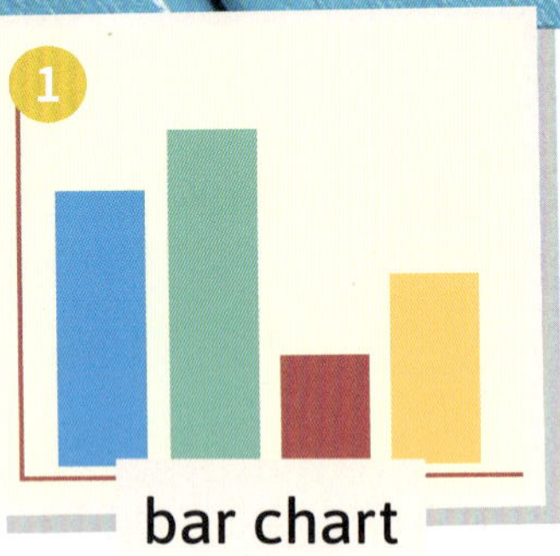
bar chart

2 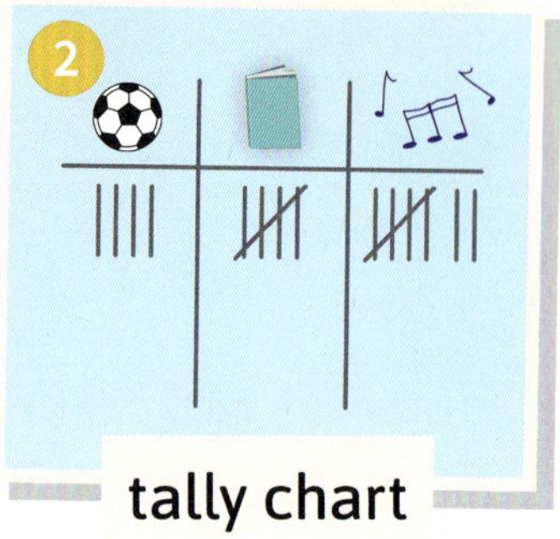
tally chart

3 
computer games

4 
films

**2** Look at the key and colour the bar chart.

How many children like ... ?

**3** Look at the bar chart. Complete the tally chart.

| Do you like ...? | |
|---|---|
| playing football | IIII |
| watching films | |
| playing computer games | |

## 4 Project Make a bar chart about your friends.

a Ask questions and complete the tally chart:

Do you like reading?

Yes, I do.

| Do you like ...? | |
|---|---|
| reading  | |
| swimming  | |
| dancing  | |

b Now draw a bar chart using the numbers on the tally chart.

c Colour the bars.

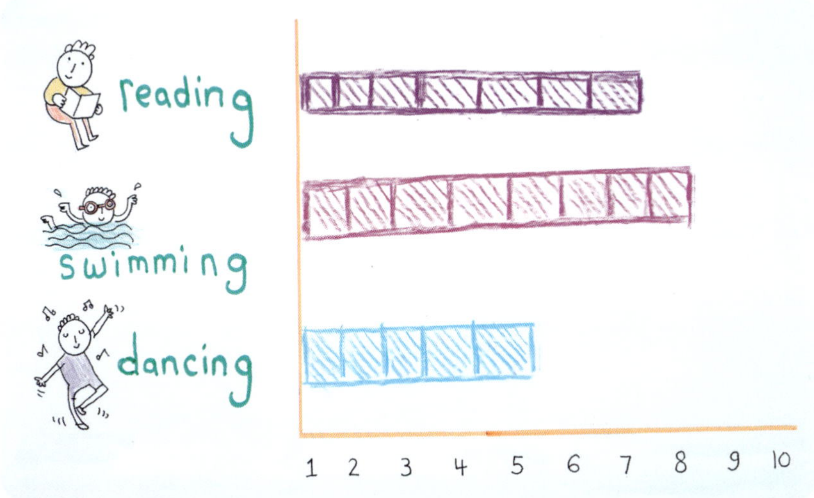

1 106 Listen and imagine. Then draw your picture.

2 Show your picture to your friend. Say.

## 1 Read and match.

1 
2 
3 
4 

swim play football read paint

## 2 Complete.

1 

_____Are_____ you running?
Yes, I am.

2 

Are you running?
No, __________
__________.

3 

Are you __________ football?
Yes, ______ ______.

## 3 Read and count. Write the numbers.

1 

☐

2 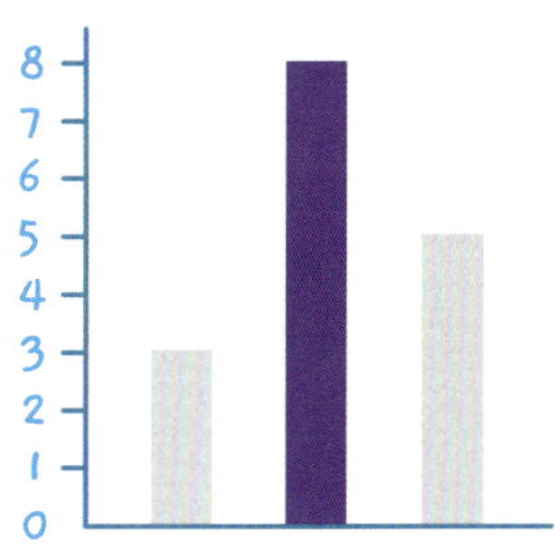

☐

3 

☐

# The alphabet

1 107 Look, listen and say.

a b c d

j k l m

s t u v

e f g h i

n o p q r

w x y z

# 1 My classroom

**1** 108 **Look, listen and say. Trace and colour.**

1

2

3

4

5

# 2 My body

1 (109) **Look, listen and say. Trace and colour.**

1

**How many** eyes have you got?

**I've got** three eyes.

2

**How many** heads have you got?

**I've got** two heads.

3

**How many** noses have you got?

**I've got** five noses.

# 3 My family

## 1 110 Look, listen and say. Trace and colour.

1

2

# 4 At the zoo

## 1 111 Look, listen and say. Trace and colour.

1

2

# 5 My food

1 112 Look, listen and say. Draw or .

1

2

3

4

# 6 My town

## 1 113 Look, listen and say. Trace the words.

1

There's a park.

2

There are two cinemas.

3

Where's the park?

It's there.

4

Where's the cinema?

It's there.

# 7 Jobs

1 114 Look, listen and say. Trace the words.

1

Is he a fire fighter?

No, he isn't.
He's a gardener.

2

Is she a doctor?

No, she isn't.
She's a gardener too.

# 8 My clothes

**1** 115 **Look, listen and say. Trace the words.**

Is he wearing a coat?

No, he isn't.

Is she wearing a scarf?

Yes, she is.

I'm wearing my hat!

# 9 My hobbies

**1** 116 **Look, listen and say. Trace the sentences.**

I'm swimming.

I'm running.

Are you running?

No, I'm not.

Are you dancing?

Yes, I am.

UNIT 1 page 11

UNIT 2 page 25

2 3 4 4

UNIT 3 page 33

UNIT 4
page 41

UNIT 5
page 51

UNIT 6
page 66

UNIT 7
page 76

UNIT 8
page 83

UNIT 9
page 93